The Art of Following

The Art of Following

Building the Foundation for the
Leadership Pyramid

Jennifer Streeter

To order additional copies of this book, contact:
Xlibris Corporation
1-888-795-4274
www.Xlibris.com
Orders@Xlibris.com
60841

Contents

Acknowledgments

Writing a book takes more courage and dedication than I first anticipated. After talking to many colleagues and reflecting for inspiration, the idea came to me that we focus a lot of time and energy on how to develop employees for the good of the organization but rarely do we develop the actual person inside. I have taken an approach to leadership that reflects the behaviors of employees in the twenty-first century. This newest generation of workforce entrants needs to reflect on who they are as a person before they can focus on others around them. Given all of my observations and mentoring of staff, I am ready to share my message with others that are in similar positions that I have been in.

There are so many people that I want to thank in helping put this book together. First, to my family who has stood by me through the entire process. I couldn't have done this without them. Next, to all of my friends who gave me inspiration to keep going with a message that I believe in. Finally, to all the mentors I have had along the way. I will never forget what you taught me. This book demonstrates for me that anything is possible.

Learning to follow before you lead is the foundation of the Leadership Pyramid.

Part I

Introduction

Leading people in today's fast-paced environment is not always easy. While leadership positions are clearly defined by organizational structures, leading is characterized by how people feel about following you personally and professionally through good times and bad. Employees have expectations of their leaders. For right or wrong, they judge their leaders every day and in every action, and they share their thoughts and feelings with others.

But leading is more than a popularity contest. Not only are leaders judged on how well they understand and empathize with their employees, they must understand and be proficient in the core job function of their employees. Employees will question why they should follow a leader who doesn't even know what they do. They may ask, "How do I know my leader has my best interest at heart?" A leader may have the purest intentions, but perception is reality. Any misperception of a leader by an employee can lead to credibility issues. Without credibility, it is difficult, if not impossible, for an aspiring leader to motivate people to follow him or her.

As you read, you may begin thinking of times when you worked with leaders both superb and abysmal. Perhaps you hoped that the great ones would always be there, and you couldn't escape the bad ones fast enough. What behaviors did they exhibit that brought about those feelings? How did those feelings affect your ability to follow those leaders? What did others say about those leaders around the water cooler? Did you keep in touch with those leaders that inspired you? Would you work for that person again?

I am sure that you have several memories racing through your head. You may remember names or see faces of people that you haven't thought of for quite a while. You may remember specific situations that made you feel a particular way or phrases that will always stay with you. This is the impact experience has as your career grows. If you are just beginning a career, you may have experiences with a teacher, a friend, or someone else in your life that had the same impact. Leaders aren't created in corporations after all.

As you reflect on these memories, ask yourself, "Was that person a good follower?" Did he or she understand the importance of being both a good follower *and* a good leader? How did that person interact with the leaders he followed? Was she in the dark when it comes to the meaning of leadership? We all will meet and interact with people who fit differently into each of these categories. The questions you must ask yourself are "Into which category do I want to fit" and "Would others classify me in those same categories?"

If you are curious about what it takes to be a good follower before becoming a good leader, then read on. This book is designed to help you reflect on the qualities of a good follower that will transform you into a great leader. Some of you may come away with more questions than answers, but that will only help you to reflect more deeply on your experiences and objectives.

The Art of Following is the foundation of the Leadership Pyramid. It is the philosophy that you must understand the perspective of a follower before you can become a manager that transitions to a leader who becomes a visionary. Each block of the pyramid builds on the block before it.

This book is not a checklist of tactical steps to ensure success; rather, it is a compilation of intangibles that you need to develop in order to be successful. How you develop those intangibles is up to you and the people you rely on to help you. This journey is a lifelong process of perfecting the art of following, and it starts now.

The art of following can take a lifetime to master.

Part II

What Does It Mean to Be a Follower?

Most dictionaries will have several meanings for the word *follower*. Definitions include repeating a behavior, imitating someone else, or carrying out duties or obligations given to you. Similarly, the business world does not have a distinct definition that applies to the multitude of leadership scenarios.

When asked, most people will have their own definition of what it means to be a follower. Their perspectives are influenced by their own sets of values, beliefs, or experiences. The lens through which they see the world cannot be shared with anyone else. It shapes the question of what it means to be a follower, and it has an impact on how they approach the leader-follower relationship.

Given everyone's unique perspective, some will believe that being a good follower is about observing and learning from others to be successful. Imitation is one of the key definitions of following. Still others will believe that followers are those who do not want to be leaders and need continuous direction from others. So how would you define a good follower?

Take a moment to think about how you would want people to follow you. What behaviors would you want them to display? How would you explain your definition of a good follower to others? Write your definition below to help you reflect as you continue reading.

My Definition of *Following*:

_____

_____

_____

Our Leadership Pyramid philosophy defines a follower as a person in a position that directly reports to someone above them without having people who directly report to him or her. It means observing successful leaders and choosing those behaviors they exhibit that will have a positive impact and create an atmosphere of partnership. It also means not subscribing to those negative behaviors that can damage those partnerships.

How does our definition parallel or deviate from your definition? Take a moment to compare and contrast the two. If they seem to differ dramatically, that is okay. The important point of the exercise is to establish a context for the topic. We will explore ideas and strategies for bringing the definitions closer together.

The definitions will provide you with the opportunity to refine your art of following without the need to focus on coaching, mentoring, or developing others. These concerns are the domain of leaders. When individuals become leaders, they put many of their own needs aside for those that they lead. In some cases the culture of an organization puts further demands on leaders, and there will be fewer opportunities for self-reflection. A leader may place a lower priority on honing the skills of a good follower for the sake of the organization.

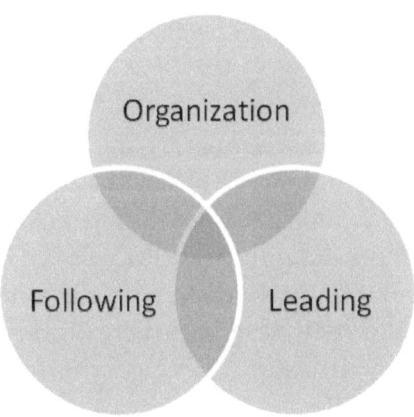

These external pressures soon relegate the study of the art of following to a secondary activity. While you may have the best interests of the organization at heart, such relegation will not help you refine your skills into the type of follower you want to be. You must balance the need to follow with the desire to lead and the influence of the organizational culture. Not an easy task.

Given our definition of what it means to be a follower, think about your organization for a minute. In your environment, what does the follower role look like? Is this an entry-level role? Maybe this is a project manager function or a formal training program that focuses on leadership development? There could also be a variety of other roles and positions that fit this description. Again, we are not focusing on those roles where leaders have subordinates reporting to them. We are focused on only the role of following without leading and building the foundation.

We are building the foundation of the Leadership Pyramid. The philosophy of this book is that a leader should emerge from those that have already held the role of a follower. This approach allows an individual to fully understand the depth and meaning of following while building credibility to be used as a future leader. Credibility is an important concept to consider while you perform in the follower role. Building credibility as a follower prepares you to step to the plate and take on additional roles that may not have been afforded to you in the past. This holds true regardless of how far you want to climb in an organization.

Whether you are considering following the pyramid to the top, aspiring to become a visionary leader, or you prefer to remain at the lower levels, credibility is the key to success. How others perceive you has as much to do with your career as your individual performance. So it follows that the time you spend at any level of the pyramid will be determined by your dedication and the trust others have in you.

It is important to not confuse the art of following with overall work experience. Some will say that simply having sufficient work experience means you know how to follow; however, that is not always true. Some experienced workers may have learned bad habits from others or have decided to take shortcuts along the way. Perhaps their experience all came from the same organization or working with the same peers and leaders. While the organization may have been performing and perceives their followers as capable, the habits it encourages may not be appropriate for other environments.

You may recognize some bad habits in yourself or those around you including taking unnecessary risks, working against the organization for personal gain, trying to fly under the radar, or even being disengaged in the day-to-day operations. Employees exhibiting these behaviors may think they are getting themselves ahead, but they are more likely perceived as poor followers in the eyes of a leader. A poor follower is a difficult label to shed. It takes only a short time to lose credibility, and it can take a lifetime to get it back.

If you do not have work experience, don't worry, it is not a necessary requirement to be a good follower. In fact you will have some advantages. You are building your foundation without the need to address any bad habits. You are a clean slate! As you gain your work experience, you have the potential to shape your meaning of following over time but be aware of how you begin.

Some college graduates come into the workforce and say, "I know what it means to be a leader, and I am ready to lead." They may also say, "I want to start out at the top. I am not interested in learning to lead from the ground up." Their new coworkers may stop and ask them, "So what does it mean to be a leader, and why are entry-level jobs not important enough for you to learn?" Some may also ask, "How do you know you are ready to lead in this organization, and how do you know whether people will follow you?"

The answers to those questions will vary. They depend on the previous experiences of the individuals or could be based on something they read in a book. The debate between book knowledge and practical experience is a constant one. But depending too heavily on one side can cause credibility and perception issues among employees. Balance is the key. If you have in your mind what it means to be a good follower, you have an opportunity to grow and learn from your knowledge and experience.

For new employees first entering the workforce, a clean slate can be a positive. Your advantage at this stage of your career is that expectations of you can be lower since your experience level is lower. There is also a perception that you come without the "baggage" that other employees may have who have been around a while. Take advantage of the time that has been given to you to take a step back and watch what goes on around you. Taking the experience of others into consideration can go a long way in helping you reflect on the type of follower you want to be.

Followers need to continuously reflect on their own skill sets before they can lead. Reflection should be an honest assessment of where you are and not where you want to be. Reflection is about looking in the mirror and honestly acknowledging those areas where you can improve. In some cases, this can be a difficult task to master. But if you take the time to go through it, you will reap the benefits.

Do I know the meaning of following?

Reflection is not about acknowledging what you already do well and simply letting go of those things that you do not. Reflection takes courage and is not easy, but nothing worth accomplishing is ever easy. It is up to you to decide whether to move forward with this process and how best to proceed. There are some ideas to consider if you choose to honestly reflect on yourself as a follower and your definition of what it means to follow.

In order to have a profound reflection on your skills as a follower, the process should include asking others around you for their opinions. These people you ask can be peers, mentors, current and former leaders, or even someone outside of the organization. It is important for those individuals to be honest with you and provide constructive feedback. Those providing the feedback must trust you and respect that you will take the feedback gracefully. The more critical one can be in his or her self-assessment and the better the feedback from others, the more valuable the result. You will have a better picture of where you are and where you need to be.

It is important to receive the feedback verbally rather than in writing. Verbal feedback allows you to ask clarifying questions about why someone feels a particular way and provides them with the opportunity to cite examples of good and bad behavior. He or she may suggest opinions on how those situations may be improved with a change in specific behaviors. For even more robust feedback, you can provide a list of questions for the people to consider in advance. This permits them time to collect their thoughts and bring more accurate feedback.

You should have your definition of a follower handy, so you have the proper context during the discussion. Remember to keep the discussion relative to your attributes as a follower. Having your ideas planned out will get you better feedback. If you are unsure of what questions to ask, use the following list as a starting point.

1. How Well Do I Accept Constructive Feedback?
2. Which Organizational Values Do I Exemplify?
3. Am I An Active Listener?
4. Can I Cite Specific Instances Where I Responded With Empathy?
5. What Is Important To You In A Follower?
6. What Behavior(S) Do You Like Least In A Follower?

List Some Of Your Own Questions Below:

1. _____
2. _____
3. _____
4. _____
5. _____
6. _____

Review our questions and those you created. Be sure that the questions you wrote are specific enough to elicit specific feedback. Will the feedback they generate help you grow into the type of follower you want to be? These questions will form the base of future feedback sessions, so you will want to revisit and refine them as your career progresses. There are times, however, when verbal feedback is not an option.

At those times, you should consider some of these nonverbal strategies. Try using a Web-based survey tool. Several of them are free to use for their basic services. You can take advantage of sending out your questions to a wider range of people; some of whom you may not have been able to contact face-to-face. Often this method allows for greater time efficiency. It doesn't, however, allow you to ask follow-up questions. You will also lose the opportunity to read body language that can provide other clues or prompt further questions.

Another option is to have a third party interview those that you have identified for providing feedback. This allows you to receive feedback without having to be directly involved. You will still be restricted from viewing the body language or asking follow-up questions; however, you will have the advantage of getting some feedback to help you through this process. It may even bring out honesty that might be held back in a face-to-face session. You really need objectivity.

Try to stay away from asking close friends and family for feedback. They can be a great support mechanism because they ordinarily want you to have high self-esteem. But in some cases, you may not get the honesty you were seeking. Even if you did, there may be some thought in the back of your mind as to whether they really meant what they said. The feedback will feel good in the moment, but it will not help you get where you want to go in the long run. While reflecting on what it means to be a follower is not a time to have your personal and professional lives collide.

You now have some definitions of a follower, including your own, and some feedback from those around you. But on the journey to becoming a good follower, you must keep in mind that leadership is not based on a finite list of attributes. It is not a checklist for you to update as you accomplish tactical objectives on the ladder to the top. The journey should be an accumulation of tools, and you are building your toolbox with the tools of the follower.

The idea of leadership is to create an environment where employees will willingly and trustfully follow you and the vision you create. There will be times in your career where you wear the hats of the follower and the leader simultaneously. There will be a common scenario wherein you are receiving direction from above, interpreting those directives, and leading those who follow you in the completion of the tasks.

When you find yourself in this position, the art of following becomes more important than ever. You will need to follow the direction of the organization and use your leadership skills to get others to follow that same vision. You will be judging your employees and their abilities to follow. You may ask yourself, "Do these people know what it means to be a follower, and have they followed the direction that I have provided?" That is the time when knowing what it means to be a follower will pay off.

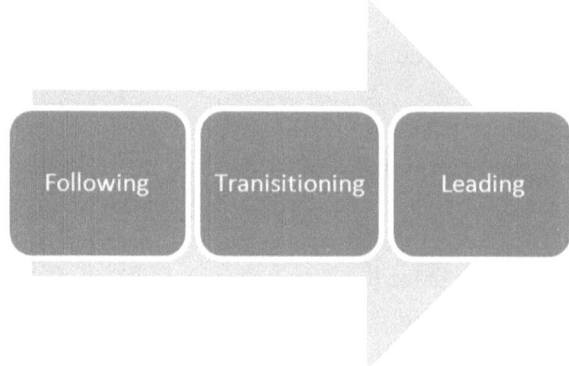

It is important to understand, as a follower, how the act of following translates throughout the organization. If you know how to be a good follower, you can work through the art of transitioning from a follower or manager to a leader and lead more effectively.

Not everyone wants to be a leader. Maybe that is not one of your goals either. Some employees find satisfaction in and excel at being a follower. One of the challenges you will face if you choose to follow the Leadership

Pyramid is the employee that does not share your desire or passion to lead. All people are not the same, and we do not always know what drives others, but leaders need to leverage the differences in people to grow an organization. Understanding that an organization needs good followers *and* leaders is a good step in understanding what it means to become a follower before becoming a leader.

You should have a good idea of how we define a follower and have taken a look at your own definition. These are the tools we will use to refine the art of following through balancing your goals and ambitions with the demands of an organizational culture. Remember the importance of selecting those behaviors that make a good follower and avoid the bad habits and shortcuts that damage your credibility. This is especially true to those of you that are beginning or restarting your careers.

Neither experience nor book knowledge alone can substitute for honest reflection and feedback. You can't know everything, so why would you dismiss the opinions of others without first hearing them out? Discuss your ability as a follower with those around you. If you can't manage a face-to-face discussion, keep the nonverbal methods in mind. The idea is to become the type of follower you want to lead. That is why knowing how to be a follower is the foundation of the Leadership Pyramid. You will tend to your ability to follow throughout your career.

So ask yourself, "Do I know how to be a good follower?" Maybe you do, but there is always room for reflection. Regardless of your answer, the next section will provide some ideas to help you become a good follower or enhance those qualities you already have.

Your definition of following is a direct result of reflection.

Part III

How to Be a Good Follower

There are followers who will always want to follow, and then there are followers who want to be leaders. Some people will follow simply because they do not know where they want to go with their careers. On the other hand, some may be happy with where their careers are at this point. Perhaps a leadership role is in their future, but for now, they are content to follow others. Still others may have been leaders earlier in their careers, so they are taking an opportunity to step back and follow for a while.

If you want to be a leader, knowing how to get to that point is half of the battle. Regardless of the path your career takes, it is important to understand the philosophy of following in order to be a successful employee. There are several steps that you should take to become a good follower that can evolve into a great leader. The steps listed in this chapter are not all inclusive, but they will put you on the road to success.

The list may need to be adjusted depending on the organization in which you work or would like to work. As you gain experience as a follower, you will undoubtedly add to or take away from the list, tailoring it to your specific needs. As you transition from following to leading, you may want to find a mentor to assist you in developing these skills. A good mentor will have seen the habits of both good and bad followers and should be able to help you recognize their differences.

After you read the list, consider how the steps align with your definition of a follower and the objectives of your career. Take the opportunity to mark up the list and add your own steps in the space provided.

1. *Understand that not everyone wants to be a leader.* If you are in a following position, keep in mind that not everyone wants to be a leader. Some of your colleagues may decide not to pursue leadership positions in your organization. Just because you are not in a leadership role does not mean that you cannot support others. A good follower can be a support mechanism for others who choose to remain followers.

2. *Understand organizational culture.* Each organization has its own unique organizational culture. Immersing yourself in that culture will help to become a good follower. It helps you better understand what is expected of you and how best to advance your career. If you switch jobs or otherwise join an organization for the first time, remember the culture is not there for you to change. It is based on the mission and vision of the organization and has developed over time. For smaller organizations, this may be more difficult to see, but it is still there. Trying to change the culture to fit your needs could backfire on you to the detriment of your skills as a follower.

3. *Watch how others behave around you.* The behavior of those around you can give you valuable insight into your potential success and/ or failure in an organization. Try to remain unbiased toward your colleagues. Realize when someone is going down a path of self-destruction and let them go by themselves. You must not try to save others to further your own agenda, but you must not undermine their positive efforts either. The art of following is staying true to the mission and vision of the organization and upholding its values.

4. *Active listening is the key.* The better the active listener you are, the more you will understand the issues around you and the better chance you have to ask good detailed questions. Stay engaged in conversations, and do not let your mind wander. Observe the body language and behavior of those you engage and learn from the subtle signals. Being a passive listener does not help you in the long run.

5. *Patience is important.* We live in an era of instant gratification and a reluctance to say or hear the word "no." In our world, demonstrating the art of patience is important to your success as a follower. Leaders are not miracle workers. They are subject to many demands, and they do not always have the answer to the questions you ask. When you understand this as a follower, it makes looking at a leadership role easier.

6.   *Constantly on stage.* In your pursuit of a leadership position, keep in mind that you are always on a metaphorical stage. Whether you are in a conversation with a peer or you are in a coaching session with your boss, your approach to the present situation will be scrutinized. It is important to approach your entire workday as if at any time you could be tapped on the shoulder for that promotion.

7.   *Don't let your appearance slip.* Leaders are always looking for followers who want to become leaders. Your outward appearance is the first thing they will see. If you want to be a leader in your organization, it is imperative that you dress as though you want the position. You need to keep your appearance up every day. In fact, it may even help to dress as though you already have that leadership position. If you think it doesn't matter, think again.

8.   *Etiquette is (still) important.* Business etiquette is just as important in today's working environment as it ever was. Remembering to use proper grammar and appropriate mannerisms is important to your appearance and credibility. Few employers want to read documents or e-mails that are as informal as a text message. Informality in a professional environment can bring your skills and abilities into question. Employ a proper handshake, look people in the eye, and avoid slang words or phrases; and you will go further as a follower with a better opportunity to become a leader.

9.   *Choose your words carefully.* Leaders will listen to what you say, judge your skills based on those words. This is not the time to be a clown or make flippant comments in a meeting. Those types of actions will come back to haunt you later. When speaking, think carefully about what you will say and how you will say it. Always remember your audience and the point you want to make. This will get you further.

10. *Be careful with social media.* Today's mobile social media tools—instant messages, blogs, and the like—make it easy for us to communicate with friends, businesses, and other colleagues. Keep in mind that these tools are used by everyone. Your boss could end up on the same site as you, and since few people use their actual name when blogging, it might be impossible to know with whom you are communicating. But that anonymity is not guaranteed. Think before you type as it could have a profound impact on your professional future.

11. *Teamwork is critical.* Teamwork is essential to the success of any organization. Whether following or leading, you must recognize

that you cannot do it alone. Being an active team participant demonstrates your ability to get along with others and your willingness to do whatever it takes to get the job done. Working on a team may present the first test of your leadership skills without a formal leadership position. It is the chance to display your readiness to take the next steps on the pyramid.

12. *Leadership is not about competition, but rather competence.* Your success in an organization depends not on how you get to the top but the impression you make on others during the journey. People respect those that are competent in their field and understand the jobs of those that follow them. If you lead others who desire to become leaders, be supportive of their efforts and provide mentorship. This is not the time to let your competitive edge get the best of you.

13. *Build credibility.* A successful leader builds credibility with employees in the organization. The simplest way to build credibility is to lead by example. Exhibit those behaviors that you want reflected in those around you. For instance, if you are kind, professional, and courteous, you are likely to receive those behaviors in return. Do the little things well, and other employees will be willing to step up and do the same. Employees don't always need the big speech to be inspired.

14. *Revive the dying art of loyalty.* A good follower will display loyalty to those he or she follows. That is not to say you should follow blindly. You should challenge your leaders when necessary, but at the end of the day, a good follower will carry out the duties a leader has bestowed upon them. A follower that has loyalty to his or her leaders will be remembered appropriately in the future.

15. *Having people trust you.* For some employees, trust is the single most important attribute for judging a successful leader. When you are a follower aspiring to be a leader, the relationships and trusts you build will move with you into future roles. Followers must be able to trust the decisions their leaders make. You must work at all levels of the pyramid to build trust above and below you to be successful.

16. *A positive attitude is everything.* Leaders will observe those followers that display potential for leadership. They watch their response to challenges and their reactions to positive feedback and constructive criticism. The better attitude you have as a follower, the better leader you will be. It's easy to stay positive when things are going well. When the feedback is negative or the challenges prove too strong,

it is not the time to show outward frustration. Look for the positive in the situation. You can be upset at home.

17. *Inspiration comes from within.* Leadership should not be about proving yourself and the worth of your skills to those around you. The same is true of being a good follower. Your inspiration is your own, and it should be found through reflection and self-assessment. Achieving goals born of your own inspiration will be more satisfying than any public recognition.

That should get the ideas flowing so take some time to reflect on that list. Use the space below to add some of your own ideas that may help you to become a good follower. Be sure to return to these lists periodically and evaluate which items have brought positive results. What might you change based on the experiences you have had since you last looked at the list? Revisiting the list will help you see how your perspective of a follower has changed over time.

Add your own list here:

1. _____
   _____
2. _____
   _____
3. _____
   _____
4. _____
   _____
5. _____
   _____
6. _____

If you look at all of the items on this list and think about the time it takes to build these skills, incorporating what you have added, you will realize that being a good follower does not come overnight. There is no magic dust that sprinkles over you while you sleep, suddenly waking you with all of the answers. The process of following will need continued attention. As you go through your career, you will continue to refine this list and your skills.

If you are in a leadership role and you found some of these attributes had a bigger impact than others, you may want to keep those in mind.

When you find yourself mentoring someone else, you can help them refine their list. But mentoring doesn't have to come from existing leaders. You can begin the mentoring process by helping other followers understand how you have become a good follower. You will be leading by example when you demonstrate your positive behaviors.

The art of following is not something typically found in a job description or performance review. So how can your skills as a follower apply to your job? How can those skills be measured? You need to look for ways to incorporate measurable criteria based on the skills of a follower into your organizational standards and practices. This will be a new way of thinking for some, and it may require you to sell the concept to your leaders. But these intangible qualities are what separate the star employees from those that just do enough to get by.

"It's not my job" is a common phrase used by poor followers.

Part IV

Being Evaluated as a Follower

Do you know what is in your job description? Is what is written in a job description important? Does a job description define your duties and responsibilities as an employee? Does your job description define how you must behave? How often should you look at your job description? These questions are common when employees consider their job descriptions.

Some employees may infer their job duties from their titles while others may base their success and place within an organization solely on their job descriptions. They use the tasks, knowledge, skills, and abilities defined in the description as their checklist for success regardless of their title.

Meanwhile, employers do not depend upon a job description to define the entirety of success. They see it as a set of tactical objectives to measure one's competency for performing on the job, but it cannot measure interpersonal skills. Those intangibles are measured by others around you. They have at least as much bearing on your success as your ability to complete tasks.

Unfortunately, intangible skills, by definition, are difficult to quantify; and many of the skills used by the follower fall into this category. So it is important that your success is measured qualitatively through interaction between you and others in the organization. How others perceive you in these interactions will drive your success, but the ambiguous nature of perception means you will not see "demonstrates the ability to be a good follower" on a job description.

The same caveat applies to performance evaluations. Most evaluations involve metric tools to quantify your performance in a variety of areas directly tied to your job description. The metrics are usually grouped into large objective categories such as career and personal development, and they are layered with goals that focus on specific aspects of your job such as on-the-job training and education.

The advantage that a performance evaluation has over a job description is that, in most cases, the performance evaluation form allows free-form feedback from your leader. This feedback covers specific observations of your performance over the past rating period and can include anything allowed within the boundaries of employment law. This is a space where your immediate manager can comment on your abilities as a good follower. The door is open for the leader to provide constructive feedback that can help you build your pyramid foundation.

Job descriptions and performance evaluations should be tied together to provide the entire picture in assessing your success within an organization. They should address a balance of both tactical skills and intangible assets. The art of following should be one of those intangible assets.

So if following is not on-the-job description and it may or may not be addressed on a performance evaluation, why is it so important? Following is important to a person's credibility and displays their willingness to step outside of the box for the prosperity of the organization. By nurturing these assets, you will build relationships and encourage people to move forward.

It is important to understand that, regardless of the position you hold, you will not be given a comprehensive written list of all that is expected of you. Much of your success as a follower depends on intangible skills you develop on your own as your experience grows. Some of these skills include proactively asking others how you can be of help, reserving your opinions until asked for them, or even acting as a sounding board for your leader in his or her decision making.

You will have to rely on your instincts, in some cases, to determine the proper course of action. Your instincts may be right or wrong, but either way you will learn from the choice you make. An important question you will ask yourself throughout your time as a follower is "Do I carry out the directions I have been given or not?"

There are a number of employees today who, when asked to carry out a task, will say, "That is not listed in my job description" or "That wasn't written down on my last performance evaluation." What they are really saying is that they are unwilling to do what is asked of them. Leaders will then ask themselves, "Did I ask this person to do something that was illegal, unethical, or immoral?" If they resolve that their requests were reasonable, they may then ask, "Why is this person choosing not to follow me?"

In this situation, you will be fortunate if the leader discusses your unwillingness to follow with you. Do not be surprised if they ask you the same questions they have asked themselves because they need to know your reasons for refusing to follow what they believe is a good plan. When they ask, there is an expectation that you will have a reasonable answer.

Your reasoning had best be sound, or your decision not to follow will bring consequences. A leader is looking for followers that are willing to take on a challenge. Your refusal may result in being overlooked for the next assignment, and it may be documented in your next performance evaluation in the form of failing to perform specific tasks. Suddenly your refusal to follow appears as an incompetency. In some cases, it could be considered insubordination and grounds for immediate dismissal. While extreme for a single offense, habitual rejection of assignments certainly leads to the end of the road for you in any organization. None of these scenarios are in the best interest of a good follower.

Past generations had a different take on what it was to follow. When baby boomers were entering the workforce, they understood their role as a follower to mean complete the task given to you and move on to the next task. There was little dialogue on why the task was important and little debate on the merit of the decision. It was assumed that the decision was made for the greater benefit of the organization, and the choice to carry out or not carry out the task was not considered.

Today's employees need more concrete direction and want to know the "why" behind the decisions. They often need to know the when, where, and how as well. Their expectation is that they will receive specific answers to their questions and not just vague references. They want to be part of the process and add value to the decision-making process, but the manner in which the employee asks the questions can influence the perception that the leader has of the employee. It is reasonable to ask questions of your leaders, but you should choose your words carefully.

If you want to ask questions regarding the task you are given, we have some guidelines to help you get your answers. Some probing questions may be the following:

1. Can I have a brief overview of the task?
2. With whom can I speak if I have additional questions?
3. What is the timeline for the completion of this task?

We recommend that you stay away from the following questions/statements.

1. What if I don't agree with this task?
2. How will this task benefit the organization?
3. Can you get someone else to take on this task because I don't have time?

As it was with previous suggestions in this book, this is not an all-inclusive list. You may decide to add to this list after you reflect on the importance of choosing your words as a follower.

It is important to note that you do not want to ask so many questions that a leader begins to question your ability. You also do not want to make it difficult for your leader to choose you for a task. Try to remain positive about the task that is asked of you because a positive attitude goes a long way toward your success.

Whether or not you agree with the decisions of those to whom you report, you need to find a way to make peace with the decision and support it—as long as you are not asked to do something that is illegal, unethical, or immoral. If you don't, it is probable that you will find it difficult to move into the next phase of your career as a leader in that organization. Organizations look for and rely on those followers with a "can do" attitude.

When you are a manager in an organization with people above and below you, the challenge is greater. But you will also have more opportunity to be involved in the decisions and ask questions of your leaders. Still, if you do not support the decision of those above you, it can be difficult to work your way up the pyramid. It is a pivotal moment in your career to define yourself as a follower and set the example for those following you.

If you cannot reconcile what is being asked of you with what you see as the best interest of the organization, you may need to reflect on how you fit in the organization. Your skills as a follower can only take you so far if you are constantly at odds with the organizational culture. Here are some things to consider as you reflect:

1. Are my values comparable or in contrast to those of the organization?
2. Is this an organization that I can stand behind if someone outside of the office asks me what it is like to work here?
3. How long do I expect to work here?
4. Is it time for me to move on or buckle down and get to work?
5. How will people perceive me if I refuse to follow but decide to stay?

We have provided some space below for you to add your own ideas if you are currently contemplating a change. If this is not an area of need for you, please move on and leave the space blank. You can come back and use this space in the future if you find yourself reflecting on the values of your organization.

Add your own list here:

1. _____
   _____
2. _____
   _____
3. _____
   _____
4. _____
   _____
5. _____
   _____
6. _____

Honing your skills as a follower is a part of your job no matter what your title. It does not have to be on a job description or a performance evaluation to be valid. The quantifiable skills those formal documents define are only one component to be balanced with the intangible attributes you bring to an organization. Looking outside of the box at the whole employee is an important aspect of following and leading. Sometimes you need to step out of your comfort zone and trust the decisions of your leaders, but you should not hesitate to ask some probing questions. Just remember to choose your words carefully and consider how your questions reflect on your ability to perform your tasks.

Define your own leadership style and allow it to evolve over time.

Part V

Why Following before Leading Is Important

"I want to be a leader not a follower, so how important is following really?" There are some who will take the position that following is not important if they want to be a leader. In fact, if you have already made it into a leadership position, you are right where you want to be.

Perhaps you feel that following comes naturally to everyone, so why worry about it? There are others that will say everyone is a follower in some way regardless of their position and that as children we learned how to follow our parents. But our philosophy is that there are aspects of following that we all need to learn or relearn before we can truly lead.

Whatever you believe, it is important to understand that not everyone may know how to properly follow. The role models they have had may not have demonstrated good examples of following. Some people may have had leaders that expected people to blindly follow their every command without question. Still others may have been in previous situations where following was not emphasized at all.

Think back to previous positions you have held and ask yourself whether following was important. Were you aware that you were following others in order to advance your career? Do you remember seeing references to following on your performance evaluation, or did you receive positive or constructive feedback focused on your ability to follow? In most cases, leaders will focus on your skill in the tactical areas of the job and overlook the art of following.

Some people will want to step right into a leadership role without learning to properly follow. They rely on the theory of leadership found in a book to carry them right into a management career. They may not have the patience for following because they see it as a tedious and unnecessary act. This is an unfortunate approach because they will lack the perspective that experience can bring.

These individuals tend to be younger workers coming straight out of college. They have heard their professors lecturing on leadership and figure that it cannot be that difficult to do. Leading is about giving direction and having other people listen to you. You cannot be successful without creating credibility among your followers and earning the respect of those who will follow you.

Organizations tend not to put people into leadership positions when they have not held a position previously where they have demonstrated the art of following. They understand the credibility issues that would result, and they do not want unnecessary conflict in the organization. It can be a matter of common sense. Organizations may not realize that they are looking for these traits, but what they are looking for is someone who can follow and follow well.

We know that in our hurried world people like to move through stages at light speed, taking short cuts and modifying the playing field. However, we have some advice when it comes to your career.

Don't be in a hurry. There is an old saying that good things come to those who wait, and this is especially true of leadership and the act of following. If you think about where you are in the life cycle of your career and how many more years you have to work, there are many things you can learn along the way. Following is that beginning step in the career life cycle and, as we have mentioned before, is the foundation of your pyramid.

Being an emerging leader provides the opportunity to have balance between theory and practical application. As a follower, you get a chance to try out your leadership skills on people without causing irreparable harm to your or their careers. If an action or comment is made by mistake, most likely that can be easily fixed.

Once you step into that leadership role, the stakes become higher, and it may not be as easy. The statements you make carry more weight, and the actions you take are carefully scrutinized. Whether you realize it or not, everyone is watching.

A good follower focuses on following before leading. You have a chance to look at some of the leaders in your organization and ask, "Is that the kind of leader I want to be?" Observing the actions and behaviors of leaders allows the employee to learn from the successes and failures of others. He or she may ask, "What do these leaders do well, and what do they not do well?"

As a follower, you may also look at several leaders and decide that you want to take a little bit from several people. There are also traits you would like to leave behind. Keep in mind that even if there are certain behaviors you like or don't like, they can still be tweaked so that they fit your personality. Our advice is to pick and choose. Go ahead and choose the ones you like and let them be your starting point.

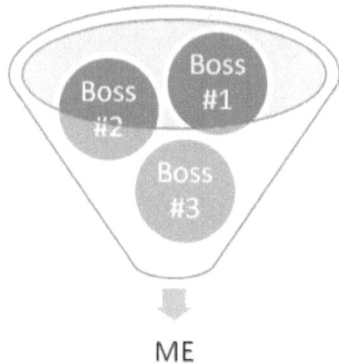

ME

Keep a journal of your leadership ideas so you can review them from time to time. Through this process you will be defining your own leadership style. You should be reflecting on why people will want to follow this style of leadership. This strategy will help you evolve your skills as a follower and leader but refrain from putting a label on your style. The actions are more important than the name, and naming your style can distract followers.

Keep in mind that you cannot take someone else's leadership style and make it your own. That never works. There will be aspects of that style that do not fit you, and your resulting style will feel clunky and confusing to your followers. They may not be clear on the vision you have and will start to doubt your skills. That doubt, in turn, will creep into your own thoughts and make you unsure of your true skill and ability. This is another time to step back and reflect. You do not want to be second-guessing your skills at this time.

As you reflect on the idea of being a successful leader, you should revisit whether you know what it means to be a follower. What further defines good following in your organization? Do they even endorse the art of following or acknowledge the benefits of having good followers? If you are unsure, ask some of your leaders. Perhaps the organization hasn't even considered following as an art. They never will if no one asks the questions that begin the dialogue. Asking allows you to gain clarity on the role of the follower within your organization.

Building your Leadership Pyramid is a learning process, and you will have many questions—sometimes more questions than answers. But as a leader, you will not always have the answer to every question. By mastering the art of following before becoming a leader, you will have a better perspective and be better prepared when your followers present these questions. The accumulation of your experience, study, and thoughtful reflection on the art of following will prepare you for success.

*Defining your own leadership style
takes courage and reflection.*

Part VI

Take the Next Steps

Once you have refined your skills at the art of following and looked at why it is important to follow before leading, you can now ask yourself, "Do I want to be a leader?" If the answer to that question is yes, then you must make some introspective decisions to get yourself there.

The answers may not come to you overnight. Most likely, you will not wake up in the middle of the night with an epiphany. It takes to reflect on the past to determine your future. As you are reflecting on your next steps, think about the questions below. These questions may not help you come to a decision, but they can be a good first step in the process.

1. *Is this the organization in which I want to lead?* If the organization is not a good fit for your style, you may think about moving on before you take on a leadership role. While this may seem like a step back, it actually can be a step forward.
2. *Do I like mentoring people?* Mentoring, whether formal or informal, is a key component of leading others. Employees expect to receive mentoring from their leaders. The bottom line is you need to take a selfless approach. You have to like people and enjoy spending time with others and helping them grow into their positions.
3. *Am I technically proficient in my position?* Being technically proficient does not guarantee being a good follower or a good leader, but it can make the transition easier. It can also lend credibility to you as a person and help you gain the respect of others.
4. *Will I have the drive to be successful in both good times and bad?* Being a leader in good times can be easy because people are happy and you

can give them what they want. In bad times, though, choices are tough, people are not happy, and it takes an inner strength to stay in the game. You need to know if you have the resolve to take the bad with the good.

5. *Why will others want to follow me?* Some will follow you only because it is required of your respective positions. Others will follow based on your personality and the understanding that you have the knowledge to get them there. Either way, you need to know that not everyone will be happy or agree with you all of the time.

6. *What happens if I fail?* While it is important to focus on the positive, you should also make sure you know how you will feel if this doesn't work out. You need to ask yourself if you would be willing to go back to a lower position and learn some additional skills to try again in the future. Think about how you want to approach the second chance.

7. *Am I confident enough to make the adjustment from a follower to a manager?* Like the art of following, the art of transitioning from one role to the next can be a challenge. When moving into a new role, you must have confidence in yourself. That inner confidence will transfer to those around you. Know that you may not always make the best decision, but when you make a decision given everything you know, you have done the best you can do.

8. *Am I a risk taker?* When thinking through next steps, assessing your risk tolerance is important. Leaders hold positions where the decisions they make have a level of risk attached to them. You will need to understand your degree of risk tolerance and the accountability that goes with decision making.

9. *Am I doing this for the right reasons?* Leading people should not be about making all of the decisions or telling people what to do. It should be about using your skills to influence people for the right reasons and being rewarded with internal gratification.

If many of your answers to the questions listed above is no, you may not be ready to step into the next phase. By this point, you have been through an honest reflective evaluation of yourself. Answering no reveals that you know what you want from your career and have not fallen to the pressure of your peers or your organization to step into a role with which you are not comfortable. It shows the confidence you have in the direction of your career, so stay the path.

Yet if you answered yes to the majority of the questions, then you know that leadership is in your future. Take the advice in this book, understand who you are as person, reflect often, change with the tide, and don't give up.

We have helped you discover what it means to be a follower, what it takes to be a follower, and why it is important to follow before leading. The better the follower you are, the more potential you will have to be a good leader. Now you need to choose the door through which you wish to walk.

As demonstrated throughout this book, it is important to understand that theory isn't everything. Practicing what you know can, in some cases, be even more important. Successful leaders need to have the benefit of being a follower first without the responsibility for others underneath them.

Once you have been a follower, you will empathize with what your followers will experience when you lead them. It will be easier to lead them with credibility and grace when you have been in their shoes than to step in unaware and hope it works out.

When you follow before you lead, you are building the foundation of your Leadership Pyramid. That solid foundation will make you stronger as you climb the levels throughout your career. Having mastered the art of following, you are prepared to take on the challenging art of the manager.

Learning to Lead from the Ground Up

Pyramid Leadership is a philosophy that evolved from research and observation of successful leaders that have worked their way from the rank and file of frontline employees. During their journeys, these visionaries will have consciously or subconsciously traversed all levels of the pyramid. At the pinnacle, they will guide successful organizations and inspire new generations of leaders.

The Pyramid Leadership model assists employees that want to become successful leaders but are not sure how to get started. It provides them with a road map for beginning on the path and successfully navigating the challenges along the way.

Sapphire Training and Consulting—Mining Leaders from Followers and Polishing Leaders into Visionaries

When the term mining is discussed in the corporate world, it is generally used in the context of data or knowledge. Few people would apply the term to the employees. Sapphire Training is predicated on the philosophy that the best talent can be mined from an organization's employee base. But those hidden "gems" must not only be proficient in their duties, they must become effective followers.

Leading from the ground up emphasizes building a solid foundation for the pyramid before navigating to the top. Even experienced leaders can benefit from reflection before continuing their journey as a fresh perspective and focus on principles can sharpen their vision. In an era of change, successful leaders adapt not only to their environment but to the criteria upon which their success in an organization and industry is judged.

Index

www.ingramcontent.com/pod-product-compliance
Lightning Source LLC
Chambersburg PA
CBHW021932170526
45157CB00005B/2284